# WILD ONES
# ELEPHANTS

by JILL ANDERSON

NorthWord
Minnetonka, Minnesota

In the shadowy morning light,

elephants greet each other by gently touching noses.

For animals this big, **it's always mealtime.**

And elephants have a special tool to help them eat and drink.

**Can you guess what it is?**

It's a trunk! It is made up of hundreds of muscles— and no bones.

A trunk works like a hand to reach for leaves and grass, or like a straw to suck up water.

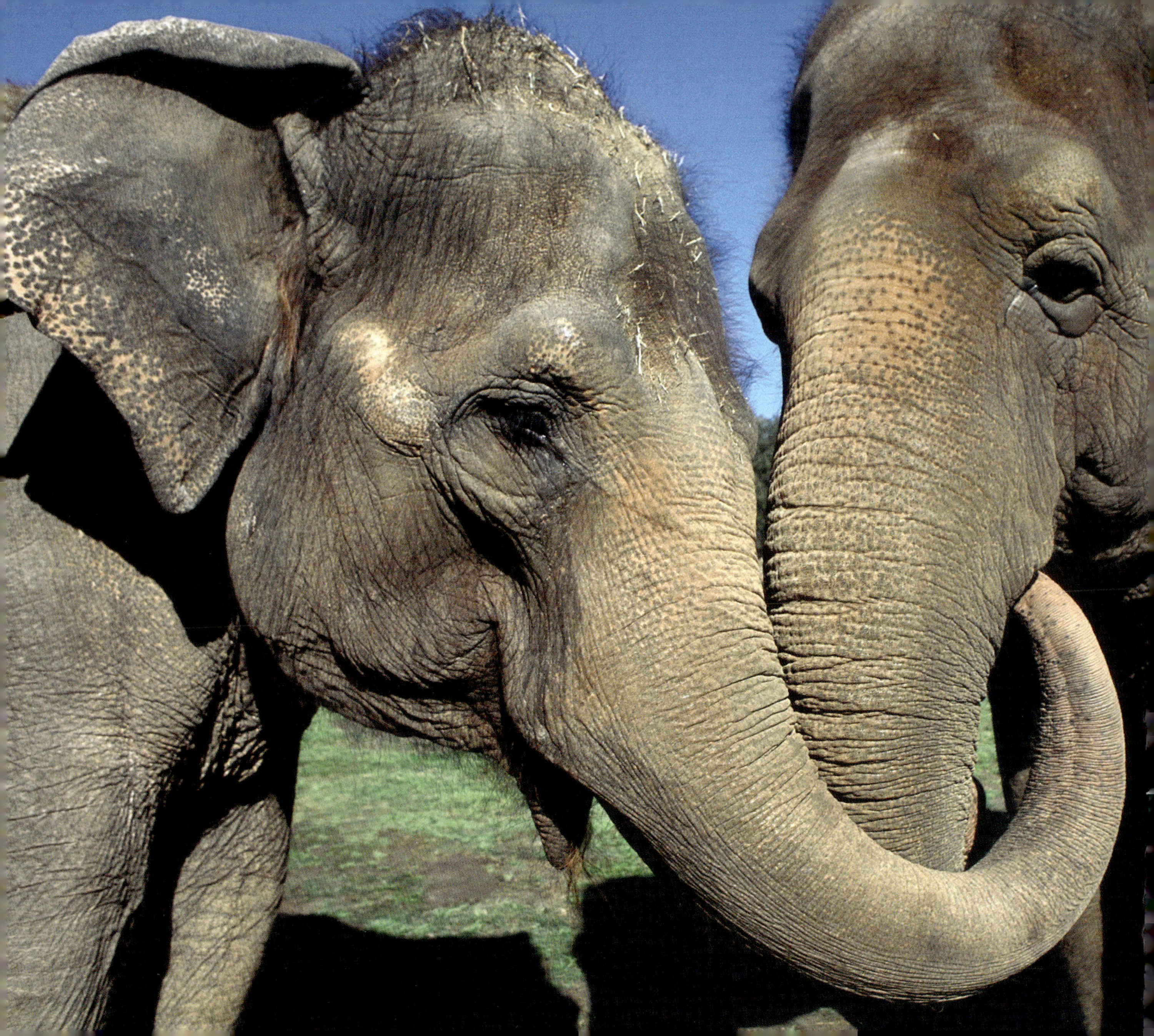

An elephant also uses its trunk to breathe, smell, and shower.

A touch with the trunk can tell another elephant, "I'm sorry you're sick" or "Let's go!"

Tusks come in handy at mealtimes, too. They are good for loosening tree bark and digging up tasty roots.

But not every elephant is lucky enough to have tusks.

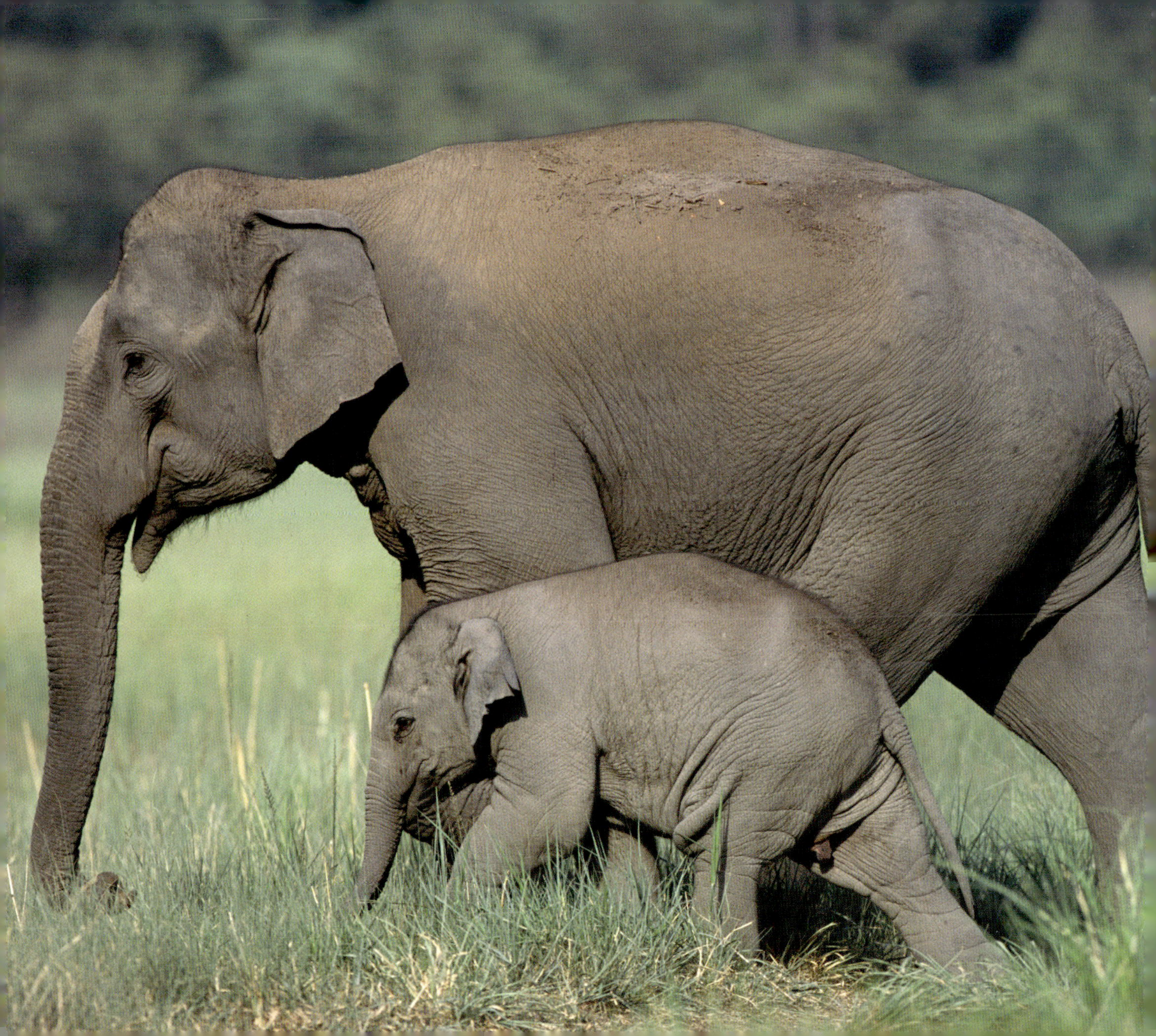

In Asia, male elephants
have tusks, but females don't.
Other ways to recognize
an Asian elephant are its
**small ears**
and
**rounded back.**

African elephants all have tusks. They are bigger than their Asian cousins.

Their ears are wide and floppy, and their back dips down in the middle.

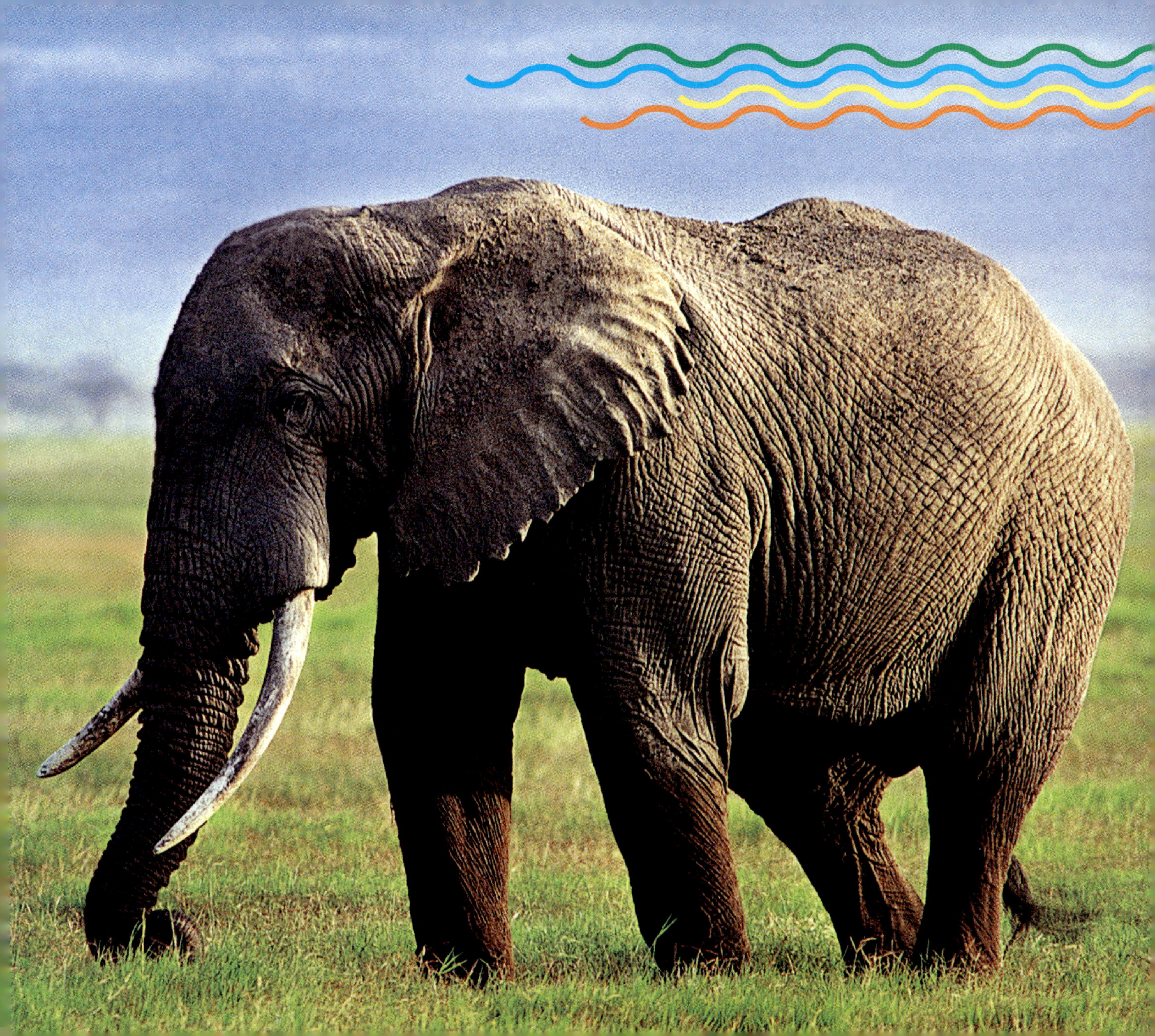

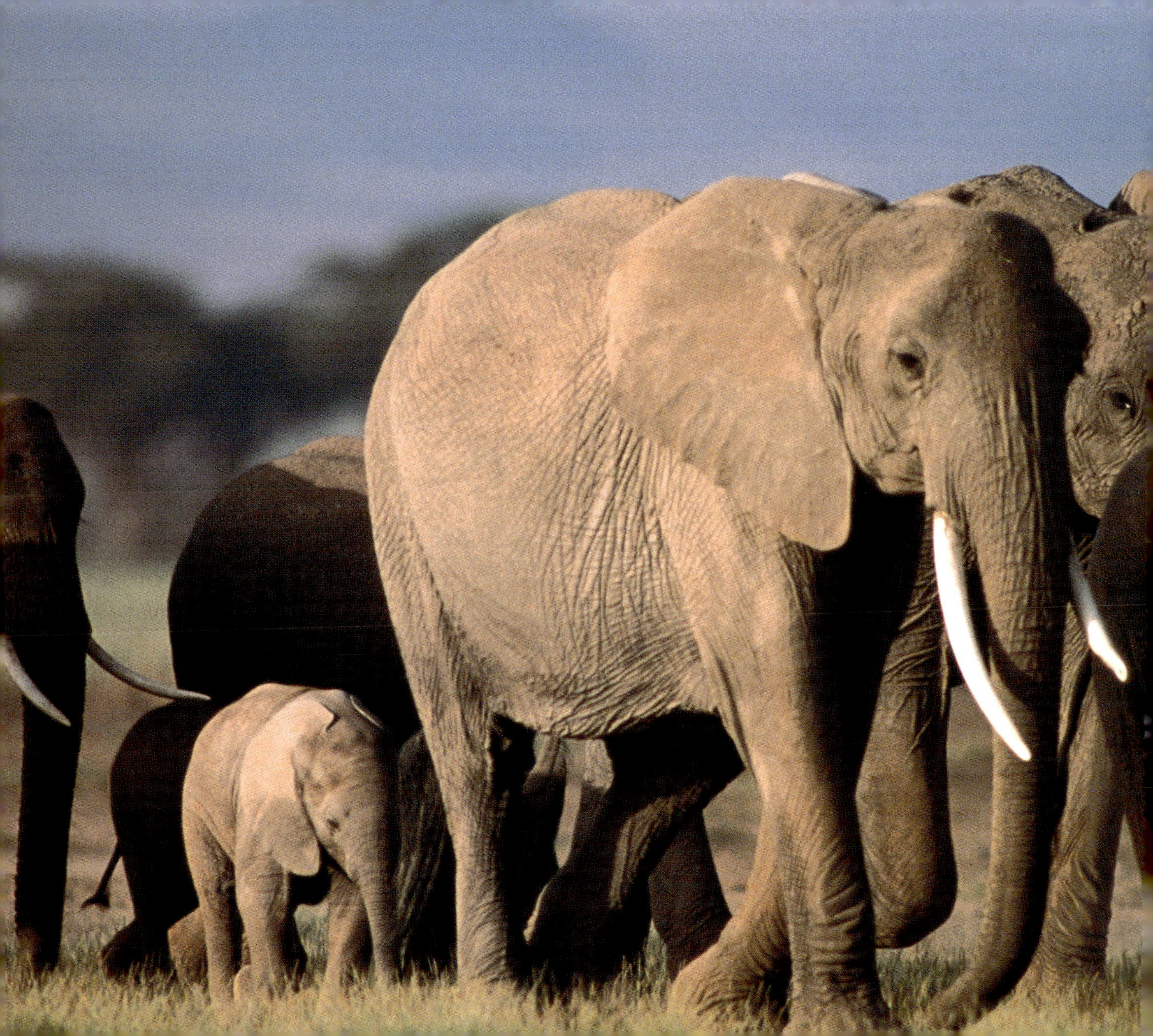

No matter where they live, the females, or cows, travel in family groups called herds.

The oldest cow is the leader. Adult males, called bulls, live alone.

Elephant cows give birth to one baby, or calf, at a time.

The calf's mother and other members of the herd help it to stand up and take its first drink of milk.

When it is old enough and brave enough to leave its mother's side, the calf plays in a wiggly pile with its elephant cousins.

When the day turns hot, the elephants find some cool mud or a shady spot to rest.

But soon they will be on their way again, looking for their next leafy meal.

*To the Jacobsen women—
a warm and caring herd who prefer
chocolate to greenery*
—J. A.

Composed in the United States of America
Designed by Lois A. Rainwater • Edited by Kristen McCurry

Text © 2006 by Jill Anderson

**NORTHWORD**
Books for Young Readers
11571 K-Tel Drive
Minnetonka, MN 55343
www.tnkidsbooks.com

All rights reserved. No part of this work covered by the copyrights herein
may be reproduced or used in any form or by any means—graphic, electronic or
mechanical, including photocopying, recording, and taping of information on storage
and retrieval systems—without the prior written permission of the publisher.

Photographs © 2006 provided by:
Penny Boyd/Alamy: cover; Holger Ehlers/Alamy: p. 1; Denver Bryan/Alamy: p. 19;
Digital Vision: back cover, endsheets, pp. 2-3, 5, 10, 14-15, 22-23, 24; Yva Momatiuk/John Eastcott/Minden Pictures: p. 4;
San Diego Zoo/Minden Pictures: pp. 8-9; Gerry Ellis/Minden Pictures: pp. 16-17;
Gerry Ellis/Globio/Minden Pictures: pp. 20-21; Galina Barskaya/istockphoto.com: p. 6; Tom & Pat Leeson/ardea.com: p. 7;
Chris Harvey/ardea.com: p. 11; Jagdeep Raiput/ardea.com: p. 12; JupiterImages Corporation: p. 18.

Library of Congress Cataloging-in-Publication Data

Anderson, Jill.
Elephants / by Jill Anderson.
p. cm. -- (Wild ones)
ISBN 1-55971-950-8 (hardcover) -- ISBN 1-55971-951-6 (softcover)
1. Elephants--Juvenile literature. I. Title.

QL737.P98A54 2006

599.67--dc22

2005038015

Printed in Singapore
10 9 8 7 6 5 4 3 2 1